GW00545345

"Sacred cows make the best hamburger."

MARK TWAIN

The Dubliner 100 Best Restaurants 2009
Edited by TREVOR WHITE
Photography by YURI IGOSHEV and GIITA HAMMOND
Design by FIACHRA MCCARTHY

First edition, published November 2008

ISBN 978-0-9542188-7-4

The Dubliner
IRELAND'S BEST CITY MAGAZINE

Published by *The Dubliner* magazine,
23 Wicklow Street, Dublin 2, Ireland.
T: (3531) 635 9822. E: editor@thedubliner.ie.
W: www.thedubliner.ie

The Dubliner

100 BEST
RESTAURANTS

EDITED BY TREVOR WHITE

FOREWORD

Santa Rita is delighted to sponsor this guide to Dublin's 100 best restaurants. The connection between Ireland and the celebrated Chilean winemaker is older than you might imagine. In 1814, during the Chilean struggle for independence, the son of a Sligo-born engineer, Bernardo O'Higgins, took refuge from Spanish troops at the Santa Rita Casa Real.

Nearly 200 years later, Ireland provides an equally warm welcome to Santa Rita. The best-selling Chilean wine in the country, its spectacular success is founded on superb quality, as acknowledged by wine critics from *Decanter* to *Wine Enthusiast*.

For the seventh consecutive year, Santa Rita is teaming up with *The Dubliner* to celebrate those places that today make the capital an excellent place in which to dine. So let's raise a toast (Santa Rita, of course) to all those restaurants that merit inclusion in this guide.

JOE QUINSEY
General Manager
Gilbeys of Ireland Ltd.

INTRODUCTION

Richard Corrigan took one of his turns the
other day. I think he was saying that Kevin Thornton
is a muppet. Or was it Dylan McGrath? To be honest I
rarely listen when chefs are being hysterical. The only
time they deserve an audience is when they are doing
something clever with their hands or speaking very, very
quietly. (Question: when Richard Corrigan is trying to
impress his wife, does he buy her flowers? Or does he
shout sweet nothings?)

As a rule, asking a chef for advice on the economy is
like melting cheese on sushi: anyone can do it, but that
doesn't make it wise. Yet sure enough, Richard Corrigan
wanted to have his say. "We are," he counselled, "at the
lovely economic turnaround of the century."

Corrigan also says the year ahead is going to be
especially tough: "The theme is going to be the culling
of the restaurants. People are going to be a lot more
cautious about eating out and where they'll go. They are
going to be looking for value for money and quality."

One hesitates to say 'I told you so' (one has no wish to
sound like Richard Corrigan). But in the introduction to

last year's edition of this guide, I wrote that many new restaurants will go under, and that "smart restaurateurs are now consolidating, re-imagining where necessary, preparing for a different economic climate."

One year on, many chefs face a particularly bleak winter, having failed to make the necessary changes. And here I defer to Corrigan. For despite opening a place in Dublin at the very moment when the economy went into freefall, the Earl of Waffle will endure the recession. Why? Because diners do not want frou frou cooking right now. They do not care for structural engineering or molecular gastronomy. They want value and quality. In Bentley's, Corrigan offers both.

The arrival of Richard Corrigan is bad news for his competitors. To endure the turmoil ahead, they may need to follow his lead. Just, I daresay, as Corrigan followed mine.

That'll give him something to moan about.

TREVOR WHITE
The Dubliner Magazine

MINE'S A BURGER!

Jo'Burger

We are delighted that Jo'Burger won the Santa Rita People's Choice award this year. It's so recession chic. Nothing on the menu costs more than €13, the furniture and menus are recycled, and there's beer, DJs, a rockin' atmosphere and beautiful people thrown in for free. (Well, the beer isn't free. Maybe next year.) All of the food is made in-house, and many of the ingredients are sourced from small producers. Good on them. Burger king Joe Macken was born in a hotel (his dad, Kevin, is a co-owner of the business) and he could never imagine doing anything other than working in the restaurant biz. Congratulations to the mighty Mackens and their excellent team.

Santa Rita
PEOPLE'S CHOICE AWARD 2009

ALEXIS

From soup to chowder

This Dun Laoghaire bistro is named after Alexis Soyer, the French chef who opened soup kitchens in Ireland during the Famine. He could make 100 gallons of tasty, nutritious soup for under £1. (How? Fillers like mint, bay leaves and thyme.) Patrick O'Reilly and his brother, chef Alan O'Reilly, are all about value and taste. We love Alan's famous seafood chowder (€6.50-12.50, depending on size) which one might follow with the organic smoked haddock tart (€11). The decor is very NYC – an open-plan dining room with floor-to-ceiling windows on one side, and an open kitchen at the back. Expect a middle-aged local crowd during the week, and tie-less self-styled hipsters at the weekend.

17-18 Patrick Street,
Dun Laoghaire, County
Dublin. 280 8872,
alexis.ie

ANDERSONS CREPERIE

Wholly crepes!

A little sister of Andersons Food Hall, this creperie is tucked away in a cute Victorian housing estate (owner Noel Delaney says he fell in love with the quirky building at first glance). Inside, it tries to look 1930s Art Deco but we think it achieves 1970s *Star Trek* instead – that's why we love it. Foodwise, it's the business. Most crepes are made from buckwheat and are healthy in an earnest kind of way – try the one with goat's cheese, Bayonne ham, honey and rocket (€9.95). Charcuterie and cheese plates are as good as those in the Glasnevin branch. Wednesday jazz nights are welcome in a neighbourhood that relies more on chart music and gargle for its cultural output.

1a Carlingford Road,
Drumcondra, Dublin 9.
830 5171, andersons.ie

ANANDA

Jaipur goes south

This new addition to Asheesh Dewan's mini-empire (he's the man behind the excellent Jaipur restaurants) had a long gestation period, and it opened at a time when many established businesses were going to the wall. Yet it would be foolish to write off Dewan, who has repeatedly raised the bar for Indian cooking in the city, and made a fortune in the process. An elegant, airy space above the cinema in Dundrum Town Centre, Ananda – it means 'bliss' in Sanskrit – serves all the usual Indian fare, but the smart thing to do is let chef Sunil Ghai order for you. We particularly like the tandoori duck breast and the curried lobster. Excellent service too, and surprisingly good value. All bodes well.

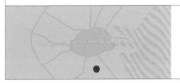

2-4 Sandyford Road,
Dundrum Town Centre,
Dublin 16, 296 0099,
anandarestaurant.ie

AVOCA

Ladies' choice

The chaps behind My Little Piebald – a scurrilous email that does the rounds each Thursday – think this lovable food and lifestyle emporium is a pick-up joint. "It may seem like an unlikely place to bag a man, filled as it is with ruthless rich women in their 30s and 40s who are desperate for either a husband or an affair. And the competition will be intense. Most of the other women in Avoca will have husbands who cannot maintain an erection without a jar of Viagra and a picture of Thelma Mansfield to hand. Hence, any man who strays into the café area will probably be jumped on." That's a fun description, if a little ungenerous. Bottom line: Avoca is a seriously wonderful enterprise. Single or not, check it out.

11-13 Suffolk Street, Dublin 2. 672 6019, avoca.ie

BANG

Our town

Let's just get this out of the way: great looking staff. Alright? At lunchtime the Stokes twins' elegant ground floor dining room (don't let them sit you in the basement) is full of grandees from the worlds of meeeja, morketing and P. Orr. They do a lot of table-hopping, card-swapping and ear-wigging. You get the distinct impression that the food is an afterthought. That's a little unfair. Lorcan Cribben does a fine steak and chips, and his Thai baked seabass (€26) remains as popular with the ladies as it was on the day Bang opened... all those years ago. Not, then, the most adventurous menu, but you'll probably have fun here anyway. Did we mention the staff?

11 Merrion Row, Dublin
2. 676 0898,
bangrestaurant.com

BENTLEY'S

Corrigan comes good

The toast of London opens a mid-range restaurant and oyster bar on the Green, where everyone can enjoy his famous food in sumptuous surroundings. You can get half a lobster for €18, the dining room is smart and the staff is superb. We particularly like the maitre d', Drew, a pantomime-pompous character who issues compliments from the 19th Century ("Nice to see a bit of class in the place"). Customers are well-dressed uptown types – your mother would love it here. What's more, Richard Corrigan's food rocks. You won't find a more delicious fish soup, and the organic chicken is sublime. Afterwards, have a drink upstairs – and don't forget to make a fuss about the model airplanes.

22 St Stephen's Green,
Dublin 2.
638 3939,
bentleysdublin.com

BAR PINTXO

Spanking Spanish

The ground floor of this Basque tapas house, sister to the Port House, is normal enough, but descend the steep stairs and it feels like you're entering a subterranean sex dungeon. Everything is painted black, the industrial shelves are covered with wine bottles, and there's no light other than a few flickering candles. (The staff must be eating their carrots – we've yet to see any major spillages.) The food is okay, and quite cheap. We like the chorizo al vino (€5.50), the prawns with garlic and chillies (€6.50), and always manage a few churros – Spanish doughnuts, delicious. Good wine selection. And you're not hallucinating – the toilets really are in the shape of thrones. Bizarre.

12 Eustace Street,
Temple Bar,
Dublin 2.
672 8590

BIJOU

Rathgar treasure

Until Monty's came along last year, Bijou was the only thing worth lauding in Rathgar (with the arguable exception of the Gourmet Shop next door). It opened as a 70-seater, but after an expansion in 2005 it now offers casual dining on the ground floor, formal above, a cocktail bar and the nicest smoking terrace in the county – complete with built-in fireplace. The food is thoughtful and well-presented. In the café bar, try tiger prawns linguini with creme fraiche and roquette (€16.50). Upstairs, the rack of lamb is delicious (€32.95). Mostly local crowd – Bijou remains one of the few really good neighbourhood joints in these parts – though a lively Saturday brunch attracts foodies from far and wide.

46-47 Highfield Road,
Rathgar, Dublin 6.
496 1518,
bijourathgar.ie

BON APPÉTIT

Dunne and dusted

Oliver Dunne's double-header has a shiny new Michelin star. It's only fitting, we think, for this talented chef has been surrounded by stars throughout his career. Before he pitched up in Malahide he had worked with Conrad Gallagher, Gary Rhodes and Gordon Ramsay. Where his peer Dylan McGrath (who also won a Michelin star in 2008 for the restaurant Dunne started, Mint) is radical and edgy, Dunne is classic and assured. Get a feel for his style with the menu prestige at €90 (€150 with sommelier-selected wine). Don't forget Café Bon in the basement – food from the same kitchen, much cheaper. And at time of press, the main restaurant was offering a three-course lunch for €25 on Fridays.

9, St James Terrace, Malahide, County Dublin. 845 0314, bonappetit.ie

BON GA

BBQueue

This Korean joint is big, brash and colourful, and it makes no apology for leaving many of its customers morbidly stuffed. The reason is an exceptionally cheap, well-organised evening all-you-can-eat buffet – €18 Monday to Wednesday, €28 Thursday to Saturday. Expect excellent rotisserie duck, pork, lamb and beef from smiling chefs. Probably the friendliest of all restaurants and eateries in Dublin 1's growing Asian quarter, Bon Ga has a real community feel. The very reasonable wine list and the karaoke booths downstairs also make it a top destination for groups, who are generally "young and quite wealthy" according to owner Mook Choi. They'll even throw in a free birthday cake – nice people!

52 Capel Street, Dublin
1. 872 7934,
bonga.ie

23

BRASSERIE SIXTY6

Big sis

In the spring of 2008 Rachel Clancy opened the more upscale Cornerhouse Grill, taking some of the gloss away from this, her first venture on George's Street. We prefer the original. We've had several good and several very bad meals across the street. And why so few vegetarian options? ("It's a steakhouse," replied the waitress before we shot her.) In Sixty6 there's a whole veggie menu – try the lentil, borlotti bean and sweetcorn cake (€12). The relaxed ambience attracts a hip crowd, but it's also the sort of place your granny would like for lunch. The mussels and clams (€8.95) are delicious, as is the apricot and prune-stuffed duck breast (€22). Don't let them sit you at the stuck-together two-tops at the front.

66-67 South Great George's Street, Dublin 2. 400 5878, brasseriesixty6.com

CAFÉBARDELI

Big is beautiful

We often rail against the evils of franchise restaurants, but we're willing to forgive Jay Bourke for dreaming of world domination. After all, not only did he save dear old Bewley's from becoming a drab department store, he also put the site to much better use than (whisper it) the overpriced chip shop it had become. A recent visit confirmed the sense of benign capitalism at work. Service is friendly and the food itself is still brilliant stuff for the price you're paying. We're fans of the spicy lamb salad (€9/12.50) and the spaghetti with tiger prawns (€16). They've recently introduced lunchtime portions – good thinking. Roll on the franchises. (P.S. There are branches in South Great George's Street and Ranelagh.)

Grafton Street,
Dublin 2.
672 7720,
cafebardeli.ie

CAFÉ FRESH

Fun with vegetables

The dining room of this veggie haven at the top of the Powerscourt Townhouse is in need of some love. When it's quiet, the spotty vinyl tableclothes on a sea of two-tops look a bit unhappy. But we're not here for the decor. Whether you're veggie or healthy or neither, you'll enjoy the food. The ever-changing selection of hot dishes can include bakes (try the fennel lasagne), stews, pies, casseroles; all are around the €11 mark and come with a choice of two salads. They do tasty sandwiches and soups, and their homemade desserts are top-notch. Service can be a bit sketchy (who's in charge of what?) but at least it's friendly. They also cater for special dietary needs – just ask.

Top floor, Powerscourt Townhouse Centre, South William Street, Dublin 2. 671 9669, cafe-fresh.com

THE CAKE CAFÉ

Obscure pleasures

Why is it that locals still seem to miss Michelle Darmody's shabby chic tea room, but folks from Howth have no trouble finding it? (Hint: It's behind Daintree on Camden Street.) Trendy young things, yummy mummies and the odd *Telegraph* reader – aren't they all? – descend upon this place for strong coffee or a sly early-evening Prosecco. The reinvented beans on toast is every bit the Saturday cure with none of the grease. True, the cakes, baked on-site, do have their off days and the staff is a bit too mellow to keep pace. Expanded seating on the suntrap patio, though, means it's all the easier to settle in with a brownie, wonder where that woman over there got her shoes and while away the day.

The Daintree Building, Pleasants Place, Dublin 2. 478 9394, thecakecafe.ie

CANAL BANK CAFÉ

Out to the wings

Brian O'Driscoll comes for the chicken wings (€10.95) on Sundays. If he's on tour, BO'D is replaced by countless pink-shirted lookalikes, with whichever tanned, tracksuited D4 hottie they pulled the previous evening. They too order the wings, get the head down and chomp their way through the massive portions in silence. It's quite a sight. Said wings are a blatant 'homage' to Elephant and Castle; the matchstick fries are no less original, and just as tasty. The best time to visit is at brunch o'clock on a Saturday; there's no queue. We usually go for the fish special or the asparagus and goats cheese omelette (€12.95). Don't forget the cookies-and-cream cheesecake (€7.95) – sweet fun.

146 Upper Leeson Street,
Dublin 4.
664 2135,
canalbankcafe.com

CAVISTONS

King Peter

The eccentric uncle of the South County foodie set, Peter Caviston regards himself as a seafood guru. His only-open-for-lunch dining room is thronged with the well-to-do – suits, discerning foodies, Killiney starlets. There's nothing like a Saturday trip out here with your special someone – the decadence of a three-course boozy lunch is masked by the homely surroundings. Book well in advance for one of the three sittings (midday, 1.45pm or 3.15pm), order a bottle of white and go fish. Prices are steep for lunch (the best part of €100 for two) but the fish is as fresh as it gets. Start with the crab cakes (€8.95) and then have whatever special takes your fancy. One of Dublin's best small restaurants.

58-59 Glasthule Road, Sandycove, County Dublin. 280 9120, cavistons.com

CHAPTER ONE

Page-turner

Chef Ross Lewis tells us of a gentleman who booked out the entire private dining room to propose to his girlfriend. He pre-planned a lavish menu and asked that the engagement ring be secreted in one of the first-course oysters. She said no. Obviously not great for the poor sap, but the real tragedy is that neither of them got to eat a thing. It's still difficult to get a table in this Michelin-starred stunner – the only *great* restaurant on the northside of the city. Try booking for lunch, pre-theatre, mid-week, or just plan a special occasion a few months in advance. It's well worth the trouble. Expect flawless food, a warm ambiance, wonderful service and an impressive wine list. A true classic.

Basement of Writers Museum, 18-19 Parnell Square, Dublin 1. 873 2266, chapteronerestaurant.com

CHEZ MAX

Paris by the Palace

"You'd think you were in [insert place name]" is the highest compliment you can pay a restaurant in our strangely insecure city. In this case it's Paris, though with the strings of garlic and vintage posters, Chez Max is probably closer to the set of *Amelie*. Expect solid, consistent bistro fare; efficient, unpretentious Francophone service and reasonable prices. Go for the boeuf Bourgignon (€16.50) or the magret de canard (€18) for total indulgence. There's a great garden out back and a terrace to the front for clients who are not scared of cancer. An under-the-radar choice for champagne brunch. Quibble: bring back the braised oxtail – nobody does this properly anymore.

1 Palace Street,
Dublin 2.
633 7215,
chezmax.ie

CHINA SICHUAN

Gold medal

This suburban Chinese has a new, obscure location – Sandyford Industrial Estate – but the space itself is clean, stylish and handsome. Nothing wrong with the food. Owner Kevin Hui goes down to the markets to forage for fresh delights each morning, and that curiosity is shared by the new head chef Lam Kwai Tong, who is from Hong Kong via Macau. Try his 'West Lake' minced beef soup (€6.50) or the Bon-Bon chilled chicken shreds (€6.50). To follow, highlights include king prawns in crispy salted duck egg yolk (€22) and the ubiquitous Sichuan aromatic duck (€25). Service is excellent. It's not particularly cheap, but we were still talking about our meal weeks later. Warmly recommended.

The forum,
Ballymoss Road, Sandyford
Industrial Estate, Dublin 18.
293 5100, china-sichuan.ie

CORNUCOPIA

Green beans

There is something disconcerting about the sight of a TD eating here. Shouldn't Eamon Ryan be sitting round the cabinet table? Why is John Gormley so fond of lentils? (The quiche of death?) Still, this vegetarian kitchen is not merely popular with Green Party grandees. Head chef Tony Keogh says many of his customers come in for a healthy meal after a decidedly unhealthy weekend. Everything is made on-site, and lunch specials include a delicious lasagne or a bake (around €12). We always order the pear and apple juice with a wheatgrass add-in. Beware: zilch privacy. On the other hand, the scrum-factor encourages camaraderie.

19 Wicklow Street,
Dublin 2.
677 7583,
cornucopia.ie

DEEP

Something fishy

This neighbourhood place is all about modest comfort and fresh fish. Chef Paul McNally says he takes in up to three deliveries a day from the neighbouring fishmonger. (Show-off.) If seafood isn't your bag, he also claims to do the best chicken wings on the northside. Are you listening, Porterhouse? Try McNally's roasted monkfish on the bone with chorizo and chick pea salad (€27); on the non-fish side, we thoroughly enjoyed our pork belly. This is unpretentious, well-executed food in comfortable surroundings, and the staff couldn't be nicer. Oh, and their wafer-thin calamari might just be the best in the city, never mind the northside.

2 West Pier, Howth,
County Dublin.
806 3921,
deep.ie

DEKE'S

Port-a-lunch

What's a fitting venue for a diner on the edge of Dublin Port? Of course... a converted ship container. At least, that is what Deke's was before it became a British army secure unit in Portadown. This bomb-proof eatery is now your classic truckers' joint, modified for post-boomtown Dublin. The signs are in Polish and English, with words like ryba and frythi (fish and chips) cut out on pink and yellow day-glo card. It trades under the name the Hound Dog Café, but is known as Deke's after the owner, a one-time Elvis impersonator. The food is basic; among the truckers and dockyard workers one spots the occasional punter looking for a good chip butty and a mug of tea. Arguably the city's oddest restaurant.

Opposite South Quay Container Terminal, (off the Sean Moore Road roundabout), Ringsend, Dublin 4

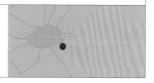

NEW ENTRY!

DIEP LE SHAKER

Swanky Thai

Diep Le Shaker was an icon of the boom. Full of bankers, lawyers and developers, it was loud. Too loud. Deals were done over plates of phad Thai, while the wives planned charity lunches with owner Anthony Farrell. Their kids took over at the weekend, fuelling up with hot curries and cocktails before hitting Renard's. Hard. While other dining rooms are feeling the pinch in more restrained times, Le Shaker and its little sister Diep Noodle in Ranelagh (which also delivers) should have no worries. The fresh ingredients, flown in from Bangkok, and creative cooking continue to draw the crowds – our appetite for exotic spices has not crashed yet. Downside? Those lawyers haven't gone away, you know.

55 Pembroke Lane,
Dublin 2.
661 1829,
diep.net

DUNNE & CRESCENZI

Branching out

Eileen Dunne says the fare is "cutting-edge Italian traditional food." Confused? Don't be. You'll find a short, simple menu: pasta, salads, antipasti, panini. Eileen and her husband Stefano Crescenzi opened their South Frederick Street flagship in 1999, originally as a wine bar. Since then, the D&Cs have opened another branch in Sandymount, sister venues Bar Italia and La Corte, and the lovely Nonna Valentina in Portobello. The original remains our favourite – we pop in for charcuterie and wine midweek when we ought to be doing something more constructive. Service is famously erratic: you may learn the true meaning of slow food. Outside is great for coffee and a fag in the sunshine.

14-16 South
Frederick Street,
Dublin 2. 677 3815,
dunneandcrescenzi.com

EATERY 120

New Ranelagh

Head chef Owen Lennon recently set his hair on fire while doing a flambé pepper sauce. His 'do was ruined, but the sauce was delicious. Maybe it's because it's that teeny bit up the road, but Eatery 120 has a relaxed, homely feel missing from other places in newly-snooty Ranelagh. Upstairs is more buzzy, a lovely place for a weekend meal with friends. We love the Library, a semi-private booth that you can book for four people. And we tell everyone about the mushrooms on toast (€8.95), which could be followed by an excellent dry-aged Fermanagh rib-eye steak (€29.95) or pork belly with mustard mash (€21.95). You can really taste the quality of the ingredients here. Don't go changing.

120 Ranelagh,
Dublin 6.
470 4120,
eatery120.ie

L'ECRIVAIN

Reality check

We once described Derry Clarke as the most affable of Irish chefs. But his appearance on *Failte Towers* has rendered the description redundant. The public now has an image of Derry that no amount of complimentary hors d'oeuvres will change. Still, his food remains; not too ambitious, not too safe. To describe it as modern Irish is surely a pisstake (corned beef with potato gnocchi, poached egg, pickled mushrooms and truffle aioli?) and the prices are special-occasion high. Despite these caveats, L'Ecrivain remains one of our favourite dining rooms. A spectacular wine-list, good service and truly delicious food are all plusses. Just don't let them sit you on the balcony.

109a Lower Baggot Street, Dublin 2.
661 1919,
lecrivain.com

EDEN

Adam and Eve it

For the last 10 years, Eden has been an oasis of calm and class in the middle of Temple Bar. No mean feat. Its slick millennial decor still looks fresh and the kitchen continues to deliver enterprising fare at keen prices. Don't let fat, rednosed barristers be the only ones to enjoy the set lunch menu – at €23 for two courses, or €27 for three, it's a steal. (No wonder they like it.) After Odessa, Eden is our favourite city-centre spot for weekend eggs Benedict; on an al fresco day, it wins hands down. Jay Bourke has, by the way, opened a sister branch in Bellinter House in County Meath, where rural is really just urban with a nicer view. If you haven't been, do yourself (and your beloved) a favour.

Meeting House Square, Temple Bar, Dublin 2. 670 5372, edenrestaurant.ie

ELEPHANT & CASTLE

It's the wings, stupid

This is probably the best place to eat in Temple Bar. Yes, that is a back-handed compliment, but cynics who describe the Elephant as an upscale TGI Fridays are rather missing the point: it's all done so well. This Dublin standard draws a few tricks from its sister location in New York: friendly service, a something-for-everyone menu of burgers, omelettes and salads, generous portions, and all of the food is fresh and made to order. Great for brunch, if you can get in. Romantic or tranquil this is not; you'll wait to be seated and have unruly foreign kids playing hopscotch by your table. But the legendary chicken wings with a cold bottle of Goose Island IPA make it all worthwhile. The omelettes aren't bad either.

18 Temple Bar,
Dublin 2.
679 3121,
elephantandcastle.ie

ELY CHQ

Wine wonderland

The SoDo branch of Ely – it's the middle child to the flagship Ely Place wine bar and the funky Ely HQ – is vast and buzzing. During the week, it serves up to 300 lunches a day to financial whizz kids and their newly beleaguered bosses. Don't panic – come evenings and weekends, things are more laid back. Start the night here with a glass of vino – bottles range in price from €25 to €5,000. Grapes aside, the restaurant menu is simple and tasty, with all of the meat coming from owner Erik Robson's organic farm. He recommends the spatchcock poussin with wild mushrooms, pistachios and orange blossom (€25.95), and for brunch, lobster and eggs for €12.95. We like. A lot.

Custom House Quay,
Dublin 1. 672 0010,
elywinebar.ie

ENOTECA TORINO

In suburbia

Our first expedition to this Inchicore Italian was on a bank holiday, when, Irish-style, all the bank machines had run dry and the credit card connection was down. Once the manager sussed that one of our party was a local, he said we could drop the cash in the next day. That tear-enducing act of kindness made us fall in love with this place. Like hippie-builder Mick Wallace's other joints, Enoteca offers good value, standard Italian fare – we like to start with the mixed crostini, followed by pumpkin ravioli (€14) or the rack of lamb (€18). The staff is lovely, the crowd young and casual. Order a bottle of red from Wallace's own vineyard, sit back and relax. What's wrong with the suburbs anyway?

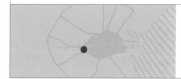

9 Grattan Crescent,
Inchicore,
Dublin 8.
453 7791

47

ER BUCHETTO

Plain chic

Fighting for its own piece of the weekend brunch pie on a busy strip of city-burbia, Er Buchetto is a quaint underdog diner that offers an okay brunch for those who aren't feeling particularly demanding. The panini and salads are tasty, and the antipasti misti are good value at €8.95, particularly when you consider where you are. Customers: chicks who chat, chew and apply mascara all at once. Staff: tattooed/pierced/dreadlocked women from Barcelona/Turin/Bratislava. Perfect spot when you've tired of the latest must-be-in dining-room and you just want to eat in (relative) peace. Pop in, pull up to one of their Lilliputian tables and order a fresh croissant and a super-strength coffee.

71 Ranelagh Village,
Dublin 6.
496 7584

THE EXCHANGE

Plush hotel

Before you settle into the ground-floor restaurant, take a stroll around this five-star hotel, formerly an AIB bank. Up top there's the Atrium, where you can take afternoon tea under a five-storey glass ceiling. In the vaults you'll find the Mint bar, good for cocktails. Best of all is the former banking hall with its sweeping ceilings and ornate Victorian features. The Exchange is an elegant dining room, if somewhat awkwardly laid out. It's a brasserie by day, fine dining at night, with uncomplicated, seasonal food that keeps tourists happy. Sunday's Jazz brunch is legendary – €58 including unlimited champagne. Gulp. Watch out for regular Sensory Dining (that is, in the dark) events.

Westmoreland Street,
Dublin 2.
645 1318,
theexchange.ie

EXPRESSO BAR

Ballsbridge brunch

With so many fatcats living locally, why aren't there more good restaurants in this corner of D4? The Dylan, Millers and Expresso Bar are pretty much it for quite a distance in any direction. Anyway, we digress. Expresso (unfortunate name) would do well wherever, but it's particularly popular here, busy at all times of day and night. You're guaranteed to spot at least one RTÉ head per visit, and the food, under head chef Trevor Reid, is okay. We like their weekend brunch; as do people who are rich enough to look scruffy and proud (as opposed to scruffy and unembarrassed, ie most Paddies). Eggs Florentine is the best thing on the menu. Fight Louis Walsh for a window seat.

1 St Mary's Road,
Ballsbridge,
Dublin 4.
660 0585

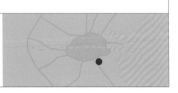

FALLON & BYRNE

Dublin's Dean & DeLuca

We love this place. The first floor brasserie is a fine spot for a business lunch. No problem with the aged sirloin steaks, or indeed the dining room itself. Very grown-up, very uptown. There is an equally large room on the second floor that makes a super venue for a drinks party. The ground floor supermarket is where rich hippies buy essentials like hazelnut truffle oil, pak choi and cinnamon chocolate from Peru. And the basement is a posh pick-up joint for lawyers on their way to the Odessa Club. Try the fish stew (€9.50) any time of day or night. (You know what? Ignore these cheeky observations. Fallon and Byrne is actually a godsend – Avoca for full-on foodies – and it deserves your support.)

11-17 Exchequer Street,
Dublin 2.
472 1010,
fallonandbyrne.com

HARVEY NICHOLS

Yummy Drummy

Dundrum Town Centre has become a social phenomenon, generating earnest analysis in broadsheets, parody in novels and even its own vernacular: Yummy Drummies and their Mall-teaser offspring patrol the aisles. Of the many restaurants keeping the natives and visitors well-fueled, the First Floor at Harvey Nics is lord of the manor. Thomas Haughton's cooking is fancy without being fussy and experimental without making you feel you are being experimented on. The table d'hote three-course menu has been brought back – at €45 it's a good way to sample a bit of everything. Don't leave without visiting the cocktail bar and the Food Market. Not necessarily in that order.

Dundrum Town Centre,
Sandyford Road,
Dublin 16. 291 0488,
harveynichols.com

THE FRENCH PARADOX

Bordeaux in Ballsbridge

The Dublin 4 address of this chi chi wine bar is reflected in both the prices and the clientele, but a flexible menu means you don't have to commit to a big spend. The focus is on wine, French, and lots of it – bottles are stacked in every available spot. Downstairs you can perch on high tables, choose from 150 varieties and sample the 'amuses-gueules.' Upstairs in the Tasting Room, owners Tanya and Pierre Chapeau have also kept the menu small and extremely French. There is a daily hot special to complement the cold meats, paté, cheeses and fish plate; the smoked duck salad (€15.80) and pan-seared foie gras (€18.95) are firm favourites. Very sweet place for a first date.

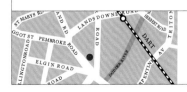

53 Shelbourne Road,
Dublin 4.
660 4068,
thefrenchparadox.com

LES FRÈRES JACQUES

Too posh for us

We're not allowed to eat here anymore. There was an incident. Let's not go into it. Anyway, we're still happy to recommend Les Frères Jacques. Like young upstart Chez Max across the road, it offers the authentic French experience, from the decor to the staff, the wine and the menu of Gallic classics. But unlike Chez Max, LFJ is posh – Senator David Norris spends St Stephen's Day here, and Seamus Heaney is a regular. Fancy cooking! Try the delicious sole meuniere for a hefty €38, or ignore the a la carte and enjoy a four-course set dinner for the same price. Great selection of wines too, and on Mondays and Tuesdays every bottle is half price. Alas, service is, well, French.

74 Dame Street,
Dublin 2.
679 4555,
lesfreresjacques.com

GRUEL

Shabby chic

This place ticks a great many boxes – price, location, crowd, food, cool factor. And for those of us on the wrong side of 30, having Billy Scurry behind the counter is a weird but pleasant treat. (You know, at Electric Picnic 2008 he DJ'd and held a cookery demonstration. What a guy.) The food is fresh and homely and the menu changes regularly. If you're working in the city-centre and you can't face another crappy sandwich al desko, grab a Roast in a Roll to go. And while you're there, you may as well take one of the best brownies in town. Weekend brunch is great, although you may have a wait on your hands, and Gruel is now open for breakfast too. Beware of surly staff. They don't mean to be rude.

68a Dame Street,
Dublin 2.
670 7119

L'GUEULETON

Post-Troy blues?

We found out what the name means – 'a big family feast of food and wine.' Pretentious rubbish? Perhaps. But when this French bistro opened on Fade Street in 2004 *everyone* wanted a piece. You couldn't blag a table without some serious effort – they still don't accept reservations. Troy Maguire's peasant-French menu was worth waiting for. Maguire left to open Locks in 2007, but Warren Massey, ex-Dobbins, has taken over without letting the standards drop. Start with the duck egg mayonnaise – it's a delicious surprise. For mains, the chef recommends the Toulouse sausage (€26.50). Plans are afoot to introduce food to the no-name bar upstairs – bring it on.

1 Fade Street,
Dublin 2.
675 3708,
lgueuleton.com

HONEST TO GOODNESS

Nice and sloppy

We're happy that Darragh Birkett and Martin Ansbro's place is up and running again after a devastating fire. Mainly because we're addicted to their Friday special, the Sloppy Joe (€6.95). Drool. As the name implies, everything here is natural, made fresh on the premises with ingredients picked up from local suppliers. Early risers will spot the trays of bread and desserts cooling in the window every morning. The seating area is not exactly lavish – though it is, to be fair, pretty – and it fills up quickly, so grab the aforementioned Joe, Thursday's homemade burger, or the very good-value soup and sandwich deal (€6) to go. And maybe a muffin, just cos they're there.

George's Street Arcade,
Dublin 2.
633 7727,
georgesstreetarcade.ie

HUGO'S

Pretty young thing

Gina Murphy's place has been performing quite well since it opened in 2007, particularly given the location (it's across the road from Bang and the Unicorn). Hugo's is funky and very *now*, with Laura Ashley-on-acid decor and a menu that keeps everyone happy – seafood, steaks, French, Italian. Murphy does a kicking lunch trade among senior civil servants, whose arms are easily twisted into ordering that second glass of wine. There are actually 150 wines by the bottle, and half of them are available by the glass. It's not the best food to be had within a 100-metre radius, but Hugo's is a welcome newcomer that has carved out a niche for itself on the Golden Mile.

6 Merrion Row,
Dublin 2.
676 5955

INDIE SPICE

Big & brash

We look forward to a new arm of Tariq Salahuddin's mini-empire opening on Capel Street – before the end of 2008, we're told – but for now let's talk about the Swords one. This big, buxom dining room is the busiest Indian in Ireland, according to its owner. Given that it's the third largest town in Ireland, Swords is ill-served; Indie Spice is certainly among the better options. Try the tandoori jhinga makhani (€16) – barbecued chicken with ginger – or the Indie Season special – two courses of the chef's selection for €15.95. Mr Salahuddin says he once sent a large order to New York for the band Soul II Soul, who are fans. There are no Indian restaurants in New York. Apparently.

Burgundy House, Forster Way, Swords, County Dublin. 807 7999, indiespicecafe.com

ome things are missing here...

ITSA4

Sandymount special

Domini and Peaches Kemp are the poshest sisters in the business, as well as the busiest, with several new branches of itsabagel on the way. But they're not the sort of girls who take their eye off the ball. The Kemps still run a great operation in this upmarket neighbourhood diner. (Disclosure: Domini was once the co-author of this guide, and her wisdom is still missed in these parts.) Service is excellent, the atmosphere is warm and friendly and the food is invariably delicious. Aged steaks, organic chips and daily pasta specials are highlights on a menu that is short and a bit more expensive than several local rivals. Nice touches like free broadband and high chairs for kids.

6a Sandymount Green,
Dublin 4.
219 4676,
itsabagel.com

IVANS

Northern newbie

Owned by the Beshoff family, this oyster bar and grill got rave reviews when it opened in 2008. Marco Pierre White was there. Tom and Paolo raved about it. Gay Byrne said it was great for the area. Georgina Campbell was ecstatic. So they know how to play the PR game. But what of the place? The dining room is somewhat minimalist, the Clarenbridge oysters (€15) are fantastic, mains are competent and the wine list was obviously compiled with a degree of enthusiasm that is unusual in this town. Excellent fish shop next door too. The successful launches of Ivans and Bentley's within the last 12 months suggests that we Dubs are finally developing a taste for seafood. Hooray.

17-18 West Pier, Howth,
County Dublin.
839 0285,
ivans.ie

The Dubliner

IRELAND'S BEST *little* MAGAZINE

JO'BURGER

Rockin' Rathmines

Jo'Burger re-ignites the teen in all of us. Old Beano comics hold the menus, long-forgotten board games (Chinese Chequers, anyone?) line the walls, and DJs, on the decks every night from 7pm, make you wanna groove. Owner Joe Macken has devised a brilliant formula: why hit a pub followed by a restaurant when you can have both in one? The most popular burger is the beef Pimville (avocado and salsa, €10.95) but we recommend the lamb Dobson (Jarlsberg cheese, rocket and relish, €8.95), sweet potato fries (€4.25) and many tissues for the inevitable mess. Everything is organic and made by small producers. We think Mr Macken should be Secretary-General of the United Nations.

137 Rathmines Road,
Rathmines, Dublin 6.
491 3731,
joburger.ie

JOHNNIE FOX'S

On high

The cynics find it hard to resist a snigger. Johnnie Fox's is, they claim, no more than a twee tourist trap. However, it has the provenance to back up the Olde Irish vibe and, more importantly, a night up here really is good craic. For 200-odd years, locals and visitors have met here to tell stories around the fire, and in the 1950s and 1960s the whole country listened to the famous music and storytelling seisúins on the radio. Delicious seafood is served every day from 12.30-9pm. If you're feeling brave, go the whole hog with the Hooley night – a four-course meal followed by traditional music and Irish dancing (€55). Note: this will be significantly less fun for the designated driver.

*Glencullen,
County Dublin.
295 5647,
jfp.ie*

KIMCHI/THE HOP HOUSE

Half and half

Half of this bar/restaurant used to be the Shakespeare pub, the facade of which is still standing. A bit of a shame that the interior is now so vastly different from the Victorian exterior, but that's progress. Kimchi is the name of a fermented Korean vegetable dish, which is served as a side, or banchan, to many of the menu items in this neat little room. Pristine young Koreans in black and white serve with a rare smile and an even rarer competence. From the massive menu we recommend the bulgoggi roll (marinated beef, rice and vegetables, €11), the crazy roll (salmon and crab, other crazy things, €13.50), or any of the sushi. Live bands at the weekends. Sake very good.

160 Parnell Street,
Dublin 1.
872 8318,
hophouse.ie

KOH

Crab-a-licious

Disco. Club. Cocktail bar. Thai restaurant. Koh has a lot to offer. The cocktail list is quite impressive and the eye candy is mostly free of artificial flavourings. The star of the menu is the soft-shelled crab (€9.75), which leaves us beaming. Other restaurateurs take note: give us something a little left-field of goat's cheese or foie gras as a starter and our stomachs are yours. For mains, you can't go wrong with the Thai green curry (€16.50) or the Penang beef (€17.50). Koh is an ambitious project and in the current climate it will have to play a spirited game if it wants to keep 'em coming through the doors. We think, and hope, it will survive the cruel commercial cull.

7 Jervis Street, Millenium Walkway, Dublin 1. 814 6777, koh.ie

THE LARDER

Dig in

We all dream of finding a nice, inexpensive little eatery with a convenient location. It must be cheap enough for regular attendance. It must be clean, warm or cool, and no dressing up. We may have found it in the Larder. Everything here is made in-house. Start the day with a raspberry scone and a cup of nonpareil Illy coffee. At lunchtime come back for gourmet sandwiches, all around €6.50, and pies at €8.50. The highlights of the dinner menu are the grilled haloumi salad (€7.95) and the beef and Guinness pie (€7.95). The decor is bland and the service can be a tad slow, but with great food at these prices, who cares? Not, then, the city's best restaurant, but a worthy favourite nonetheless.

8 Parliament Street,
Dublin 2.
633 3581

LÉON

Power of three

Still wondering why Léon opened three cafés within 300 yards of each other on the same day two years ago? Well, the plan seems to be revealing itself of late, as the erstwhile triplets take on distinct identities: Exchequer Street is the bistro, Wicklow Street is the casual café, and Trinity Street has become a full-on brasserie. Our favourite is the Exchequer Street branch, with its jewel-box decor and open fire. Scrambled eggs with smoked salmon are great for breakfast, with strong coffee prepared by lovely staff. For lunch, the croque monsieur (€9.95) and duck confit (€13.50) are popular. Plus: that chap Cricky with the funny hat often sits outside *all day*. A little gem.

33 Exchequer Street,
Dublin 2. 670 7238,
caféleon.ie

THE LOBSTER POT

Lord Byron: **"A woman** should never be seen eating or drinking, unless it be lobster salad and champagne, the only true feminine and becoming viands." If you want to look your best, ladies, may we suggest the Lobster Pot? It's warm and inviting, posh without being formidable. Owner Tommy Crean has smooth-talked local bigwigs for 28 years. The quality of the fish is unsurpassed. Try the house specialty on your first visit – lobster thermidor (€44.50) – and return for fresh prawns, black sole or salmon, all prepared in your choice of traditional style. Our readers love this restaurant, and with good reason: it's put-your-suit-on classy without being up its own bum.

9 Ballsbridge Terrace,
Dublin 4.
668 0025,
thelobsterpot.ie

LOCKS

New elite

Kelvin Rynhart and Teresa Carr's re-imagining of a Dublin classic is among our favourite restaurants. Head chef Troy Maguire made his name in L'Gueuleton before decamping to the banks of the Grand Canal, where he now prepares dishes that are by no means cheap. This is urbane cooking for rich thirtysomethings. At dinner one might start with a black pudding and apple tarte tatin (€14) and follow with monkfish in a curried mussel broth, with puy lentils and leeks (€29.90). Saturday afternoon is a particularly pleasant time to descend on the airy, elegant dining room, with last orders at 3.30pm and (usually) only a handful of other customers. Excellent service.

1 Windsor Terrace,
Portobello, Dublin 8.
454 3391,
locksrestaurant.ie

MADINA

Holy land

Beware of the glare: it's bright enough for a surgeon to perform in Madina. That is *not* why it attracts so many Indian and Pakistani doctors – they are, nonetheless, a good barometer of its culinary authenticity. The USP here is the dosa, a filled pancake which is not available anywhere else in the city. We are thoroughly addicted to the moongi dall, a kind of spicy vegetarian lentil-fest (€7.95) and the lamb Jalfresi (€11.95). Share your rice, the portions are massive. No liquor licence means the wines and beers are alco-free: the peach-flavoured lager is surprisingly swiggish. Everything is cheap! Please try this place – it's the most curious Indian on the northside.

60 Mary Street,
Dublin 1. 872 6007,
madina.ie

LA MAISON DES GOURMETS

Gallic charm

This precious little café once seemed like a strange addition to Castle Street, sandwiched between the bohemian Grogan's and a second-hand clothes shop. The sight of punters pondering life over a pain au chocolat – outside! in winter! – had passersby gawking in amazement. Then the smoking ban came along. Everything here is French. All the staff, all the wine, even the flour in the bread. Indeed you can also learn French in the dining room upstairs. (Beware: it's tiny. *Never* end a relationship here.) Baked breads, pastries and real coffee are available to take out downstairs, and they do lovely filled baguettes at lunch. Upstairs we order the fresh onion soup (€6) and tartine of duck confit (€12). Marvellous tarts too.

15 Castle Market
Dublin 2
672 7258

MELODY

Sounds good

A hundred members of Dublin's Chinese community packed out Melody to watch the opening ceremony of the Beijing Olympics in summer 2008. Most other nights it's the Paddies who fill this versatile, new-generation joint. The ground floor is a low-lit marble space with a bar, which opens out into an area containing what must be the biggest TV in the city. Downstairs in the basement a small warren of corridors lead to private rooms. Not an upscale brothel, but a place where wannabes and please-kill-mes come to croon or choke their way through 'I Will Survive.' The food is okay, though it feels like an incidental accompaniment to a good night spent quaffing and warbling.

122 Capel Street,
Dublin 1.
878 8988

LA MÈRE ZOU

Duck in

It's easy to forget about this basement restaurant as it has such fancy neighbours (the Shelbourne and Bentley's). They serve a variety of tasting plates at lunch, which is the best time to go. We recommend La Landaise: smoked duck with a French bean salad, alongside a confit duck leg and pommes Sarladaises (€18.50). Another option is l'Oceane (€20.50): a bowl of mussels accompanied by a scallop and prawn brochette. Service is courteous, and on a sunny day it's worth remembering that there are two tables outside on the terrace. Inside is a bit pokey and when it's full the noise level is alarmingly high (on Friday and Saturday nights there's live jazz).

22 St Stephen's Green,
Dublin 2.
661 6669,
lamerezou.ie

THE MERMAID CAFÉ

Splash out

People-watching paradise. Boho slackers rush by alongside teams of drunk crazies (out-of-work estate agents?) and gawking tourists. Meanwhile, safe inside your glass-boxed dining room, you are tucking into a French-meets-East-Coast-American menu complemented by Californian wine. Another odd mix, but one that works. We've had many memorable meals here in the last 12 years and have been saved by their Sunday brunch more than once. Signature dish is the seafood casserole (€32.95). Follow with pecan pie and maple ice cream (€8.95). We almost got through this review without mentioning the crab cakes. They are the best in Dublin because they actually contain crab.

69-70 Dame Street,
Dublin 2.
670 8236,
mermaid.ie

METRO CAFÉ

Bellevue

The name is French, it's a cheesy French café (Toulouse-Lautrec posters, blackboard menu, red leather banquettes) and, yes, it's full of Gallic folk. We know they're French because they're better-looking than the punters in Busyfeet & Coco next door. Large wall-mounted mirrors make it easy to spy on your neighbour. Alas, the food doesn't merit much attention. One might have a bland Caesar salad (€6.50), a wrap, a bagel, a turkey sandwich (sliced pan, iceberg, turkey. C'est tout. €6.75). Yawn. Nothing on the bog-standard menu is as cheap as the surroundings suggest. Still, they do a decent breakfast and on a sunny day the terrace is a splendid spot for ogling strangers.

43 South William Street,
Dublin 2.
679 4515

MINT

Awkward genius

You must know Dylan McGrath?

No? Well his Ranelagh restaurant won a Michelin star. And he was the 'star' of that documentary, *The Pressure Cooker*. If you can still stomach your truffles knowing all about McGrath's aggressive management style, what can you expect from a visit to Mint? A pokey dining room? Superb service? A gob-smacking wine list? Avant garde artistry? Abstract flavour expressionism? A chef who is as volatile as Beethoven in labour? All this and more. Leading chefs have bristled at his success and launched vitriolic attacks on him via the tabloid press. Yet when we asked the chefs from the 100 best restaurants to name the best chef in the city, Dylan McGrath was their top choice.

47 Ranelagh Village,
Dublin 6.
497 8655,
mintrestaurant.ie

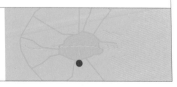

MONTY'S OF RATHGAR

Suburban spice

The owner of Ireland's only Nepalese restaurant, Shiva Gautam, is a qualified engineer. It's something to fall back on if it all goes wrong. The chances of that are slim. Monty's in Temple Bar has been a foodie favourite for 11 years, and this new branch is already a hit among adventurous southsiders. It feels more refined than its city-centre sister – maybe it's the lack of stag parties. The chefs are all from Nepal, and the food is inventive, quirky, pleasantly *different*. Try one of the tasting menus (€50-95). A la carte, we recommend the momo dumplings (€16, but remember to order them 24 hours in advance), or Gorkhali curry with lamb (€18), washed down with Shiva's own beer... Shiva.

88 Rathgar Road,
Rathgar, Dublin 6.
492 0633,
montys.ie

NOSH

Dalkey darling

Dalkey. What a strange little place. So pretty, so Anglo, so insular. We townies don't invade too often, the natives leave even less. Which suits Nosh down to the ground. It hosts well-heeled locals with their little Saoirses and Colums during the day; sans kids and avec Chardonnay at night. This small dining room is bright, modern and casual, with funky white chairs we're going to steal next time. The owners say the menu features "nice, uncomplicated food, cooked with care and generosity." The fish and chips (€20.95) would be our tip – perfect batter, delicious chunky chips, mushy peas on the side. It's not as cheap as they'd have you believe, but then, this *is* Dalkey.

111 Coliemore Road,
Dalkey, County Dublin.
284 0666, nosh.ie

ODESSA

Brunch o'clock

Quibble: since the opening of the Odessa Club, you're often plonked up there for lunch rather than in the main restaurant. The chairs are squishy, it's uncomfortably quiet and the waiters are too far from the kitchen to make things happen lunchtime-fast. But let's not carp: we still love Odessa. Everyone knows by now that it's the best place for weekend brunch. Cheap and very cheerful. Venture away from the eggs if you can and try the superb chicken quesadilla (€11). At nighttime it's intimate and romantic – our pick for a first-date restaurant. Bargain-hunters, go for the set dinner (€40), which includes most of the menu's highlights. Very attractive staff.

14 Dame Court,
Dublin 2.
670 7634,
odessa.ie

ONE PICO

Haute value

Young chefs are a bombastic bunch, feeding the press extravagant meals and outlandish boasts. Many of them will soon go out of business. They might do well to follow the example of Eamonn O'Reilly. A bright young thing in the 1990s, his One Pico migrated from Camden Street to Molesworth Place in 2001. He quickly established a reputation with critics and offered good value fare long before it became fashionable. Bold-print regulars come for the signature dish of langoustine risotto, sautéed prawns, truffle foam, sweet peas and sorrel (€19.50). Service is okay, there is a decent early bird menu at €45 and the Polo Room upstairs is a good venue for private parties.

5-6 Molesworth Place,
Schoolhouse Lane,
Dublin 2. 676 0300,
onepico.com

PEARL

A little treasure

One year after a major refurbishment, Pearl remains a vibrant fixture on the business-lunch circuit; it's equally popular among Trinity academics at night, and serious foodies anytime. In fact, it's a place where critics come to let their hair down. Chef Sébastien Masi and his delightful partner Kirsten Batt – she's the Welsh lass out front – have made the dining room warm and welcoming. Not an easy thing to do in a basement. The service is attentive. The food? Exquisite. Masi trained at Patrick Guilbaud, and that pedigree shows. Try the prawn tempura (€16) or the fresh crab with potato and wasabi salad (€15) to start. To follow you simply must have the squab pigeon and foie gras with black truffle mashed potato (€32).

20 Merrion Street Upper, Dublin 2. 661 3572, pearl-brasserie. com

PEPLOE'S

Ritzy wine bar

Barry Canny is well named: while his Golden Mile neighbours complain about overheads and declining numbers, his basement wine bar and restaurant on Stephen's Green continues to rake them in. The gentleman's club decor makes the best of an awkward layout and there's always a great buzz, even if it doesn't quite merit a comparison with the Ivy. (Spot the copycat mural.) German chef Sebastian Scheer oversees a menu that is short and wholly unremarkable. (Mr Canny does not take criticism well. The poor dear.) Once seated, get stuck into the steak (€16.50 for a lunchtime 6ozer, €28.50 for 10oz at night) or the tuna (€23.50 dinner). Good place for people watching.

16 St Stephen's Green, Dublin 2.
676 3144,
peploes.com

IL PRIMO

Obscure Italian

This out-of-the-way Italian has come back to life since manager and chef, John Farrell and Anita Thoma, took ownership in 2006. John is cheerful front of house, Anita fastidious in the kitchen. Prices are highish – pasta dishes are €16 at lunch, €18 at dinner – but it's all fresh gear, which is rare enough in this town. We like the cannelloni filled with beef, pesto and pine nuts and topped with tomato sauce and mozzarella, or the creamy smoked haddock and chive risotto (both €18, dinner). Wines, naturally, are all Italian (therefore Greek to us) so ask John for advice. Take advantage of lunch and dinner deals. And ask for a table downstairs, it's a bit more fun.

16 Montague Street,
Dublin 2.
478 3373,
ilprimo.ie

PURTY KITCHEN

Burgers and Pints

Yes, it's difficult to enjoy your dinner with a bunch of stags from Milton Keynes knocking back Fat Frogs and talking about boobs three feet away. But if you choose your table carefully, you can have some pretty decent chow in the Purty. Its more sedate sister in Monkstown/Dun Laoghaire is a popular spot for both lunch and dinner, its USP being particularly good seafood. (Well, it *is* 20 feet from the ocean.) Back inland, the pub grub is uncomplicated but decent: the seafood chowder (€5.50) and bangers and mash (€10.95) are popular, and you won't go wrong with one of the gourmet burgers – in fact, have a Burger and Pint special. Just get out of Dodge before the live music starts.

34-35 East Essex Street,
Temple Bar, Dublin 2.
677 0945,
purtykitchen.com

QUAY 16

Ship shape

Shiver me timbers! The Cill Airne was commisioned in 1961 to take passengers and mail to and from the larger ocean liners that were too big to make it into Cork Harbour. It now resides in the North Docklands (rather, NoDo). Inside, the restoration has been thorough. There is a bistro, a fine dining restaurant and a bar. We like the novelty factor, and the food in Quay 16 is surprisingly good (on a boat the viewing usually beats the chewing). Have the seared scallops with pork belly and black pudding (€12.50) followed by lamb loin with Bologna potatoes (€24.50). The wine list, chosen by manager and sommelier Rom Daniel, is impressive. Not bad. Not bad at all.

Quay 16, North Wall Quay, Dublin 1. 817 8760, mvcillairne.com

QUEEN OF TARTS

Still the boss

There was always going to be a trade-off when Yvonne and Regina Fallon, owners of the impractically small but endearing Queen of Tarts on Cork Hill, opened a shiny new branch around the corner on Cow's Lane. It's like moving from granny's parlour to your cool aunt's open-plan kitchen/living space. She has the same recipe book, of course, it's just...different. The fact that you can get a table after 7am (now with elbow room!) is a big plus. QT2 boasts a sunny interior, plus savoury tarts and sweets that take the breath away. Potato cakes (and anything on their breakfast menu) make a special morning, while the irresistibly messy chocolate scone remains one of our favourite treats in Dublin.

*3-4 Cow's Lane,
Dublin 2.
633 4681*

RASAM

Star of India

Lets face it, there aren't too many good things to say about living in Dun Laoghaire. Having Rasam close by is all we can think of right now. Opened by Nisheeth Tak in partnership with Rangan Arulchelvan (the cricket-mad dude who owns Krystal nightclub), Rasam is worshipped by giddy foodies who line up to sample the fiery cooking of chef Pankaj Gupta. Our readers rave about the Nalli Dum Korma (€21.95) – slow-cooked lamb shank with almonds and saffron – and Meen Mango Charu (€23.95) – fresh monkfish in mango sauce. Don't be put off by the location above a pub – the dining room is remarkably glamorous and comfortable. In short, Rasam rocks.

18-19 Glasthule Road, Dun Laoghaire, County Dublin. 230 0600, rasam.ie

RESTAURANT PATRICK GUILBAUD

French Ambassador

Patrick Guilbaud refused to answer our questionnaire this year. That indifference to critical opinion – unless you work for Michelin – is typical of an operation that continues to excel within narrow parameters. Critics (and the Frenchman has many) complain that prices are too high and the cooking is aseptic. They argue that youngsters like Dylan McGrath are doing more exciting things in the kitchen. We're not convinced. Guillaume Lebrun remains the top chef in town, and despite the arrogance of Monsieur Guilbaud, dining in RPG is a truly stellar experience. Plus: the service is sublime and the premises features a collection of modern Irish art that is genuinely breathtaking.

21 Upper Merrion Street,
Dublin 2. 676 4192,
restaurantpatrickguilbaud.ie

RIVA

Docklands diva

Opinions are divided on Dieter Bergman. Some readers (rich readers?) think the eccentric German is "a real character." Others find him "a bit loud." He certainly knows his Italian wines. Bergman's newish restaurant is often jammers at lunchtime. Dinnertime is less harried. The slow roast rump of lamb (€18.50) is a cracking main, but it was the spaghetti with chorizo (€14.50) that wowed us: there's something about cured pork sausage half-melted into rich tomato sauce that makes us go weak at the knees. Leave room for the chocolate and hazelnut brownie. In short: don't bother with healthy grub. Just load up on the tasty stuff, and don't buy wine that you can't afford.

1 Hanover Quay, Dublin 2.
675 3577

ROLY'S BISTRO

Steady on

Critics resent anything that's popular with the public. Daniel O'Donnell, one of the most successful recording artists in Britain, gets lambasted by the press. Ditto Roly's. Hacks can't understand why the most profitable stand-alone restaurant in the city remains so popular after 16 years. Yet it does. Head chef Paul Cartwright formally replaced Colin O'Daly at the helm last year, and there is a smart new coffee shop and deli downstairs. Upstairs, try the prawns pan-fried with garlic, chili and ginger butter with wild rice (€24.50 lunch, €35.50 dinner): the most expensive thing on the menu, but a firm favourite. A four-course set dinner costs just €42. Sit at table 10 or 11.

7 Ballsbridge Terrace,
Dublin 4.
668 2611,
rolysbistro.ie

*"Its consistency had
a strange elasticity,
but sagging too,
like old knicker elastic."*

ROMANO

Casual Italian

This Capel Street stalwart has held fast as many around it chopped and changed. You don't get many restaurant owners bussing tables, but here the man himself clears plates on the floor. Bland decor: pictures of old Italian cycling greats and dated clay tiled ceiling. Pizzas are light and crispy, pasta is fantastically fresh and – they say – organic. Spaghetti with meatballs is particularly good. The wine list is short, cheapish, unremarkable. Pasta and pizzas range from about €11 to €15. Romano's also has designated tables for one – a tiny, round oasis where you can slurp spaghetti and enjoy your wine while overlooked only by a framed Italian on a push bike. Cute. Kind of.

12 Capel Street
Dublin 1.
872 6868

SABA

Bangkok-tails

There are many ethnic eateries within a three-block radius of here, but Saba is probably the most popular. No amount of name-dropping could get you a table when it opened in 2006. (Yes, we tried.) The food is very good overall: Thai and Vietnamese dishes under executive chef Taweesak Trakoolwattana, formerly of Diep Le Shaker. But what makes it stand out from competitors is the fun nighttime vibe, funky decor and excellent cocktails. So this is a good early-night pitstop for groups. Stick with the pad Thai or green chicken curry if you're feeling safe, but we recommend punim phad pong karee – soft-shell crab stir-fried with curry powder, chilli paste and vegetables (€21.95). Delicious.

26-28 Clarendon Street,
Dublin 2. 679 2000,
sabadublin.com

THE SADDLE ROOM

Beef or salmon

The new-and-improved Shelbourne is very beautiful, and there's nothing else like it in the city, but is it a bit too popular for its own good? We've all got enough money to hang out here now – at least for one drink – which is a mixed blessing. On Friday night the main bar is full of over-anxious thirty-something women, and the din is enormous (to be fair, the Horseshoe bar remains a civilised refuge from the New Dublin). The revamped Saddle Room is elegant; John Mooney sticks to the classics, and does them well. Go for something fresh and seasonal, or the seafood chowder (€12) and a sirloin steak (€36). Sit in a gold-padded booth and luxuriate. You're worth it.

27 St Stephen's Green,
Dublin 2.
663 4500,
theshelbourne.ie

SEAGRASS

Odd-casts

There are two video podcasts by head chef Sean Drugan on the Seagrass website: one shows him preparing some dishes, including plaice and seatrout, and the other shows him making bread and butter pudding and duo of place (sic) and seatrout. Great idea. Good tips. Uncomfortable host, scary music, low production values. And why did they only do two? We have no idea. It's quite hard to find this pokey joint in the middle of the New Cool Zone, but persevere. Eat tasty tapas in the basement lounge – good for birthday parties – or try the €20 two-course early bird menu. Highlights on the a la carte menu include the mushroom, spinach and gorgonzola tart (€8) and the roast chump of lamb (€19.50).

30 South Richmond Street, Portobello, Dublin 2. 478 9595, seagrassdublin.com

SEASONS

Hot lunch

The "thinnest, prettiest girls in Ireland" come here to pout and push around their salad; their loss, since the food here is as lovely as the dining room. Chef Terry White is a capable figure, without being wildly imaginative or experimental. We love coming here for Sunday lunch – it feels decadent, but is actually not bad value considering the quality of the food. For €60 you get to hit the Tasting Station (buffet to you and me) for starters that include mussels, crab, scallops, shrimp and other treats, then choose a main course from the a la carte, and finish with a selection of desserts. Best loos in Dublin, too. P.S. One can also have a selection of vastly overpriced sandwiches in the bar.

Simmonscourt Road,
Dublin 4. 665 4742,
fourseasons.com/
dublin

SHANAHAN'S ON THE GREEN

Worth paying for

The name brings cartoon dollar signs to our eyes, but few who visit this peerless steakhouse leave feeling hungry. Located in a beautiful townhouse on the Green, the interior is comfortable, from the downstairs Oval Office lounge through the dining rooms on the ground and first floors. The waiters are gracious but not fawning, just as the atmosphere is refined without being stuffy. Have the 12oz Filet Mignon (€48.50) and delicious sides: creamed sweet corn, onion strings, sautéed wild mushrooms. (Loose trousers an advantage.) Remember to ask for a bowl of creamed horseradish, and have a drink in the bar before your meal. A place where plans are hatched.

119 St Stephen's Green,
Dublin 2. 407 0939,
shanahans.ie

SHEBEEN CHIC

Paddy ain't whack

Something of a freak. Shebeen Chic – one *must* hate that name – is the fourth restaurant to occupy this space in three years. It's the first that looks like it might survive a winter. Jay Bourke has joined forces with American chef Seamus O'Connell – and Stephen McClusker of Bóbó's – to create a recession-proof diner in the Oirish idiom. Downstairs is perfect for a party and the menu is packed with old-Irish treats like boxty, lamb shanks (€15) and bacon & cabbage (€15). Highlights include a super-bony blackened eel with banana ketchup (€16) and grilled mackerel and curry mayo (€12). Real culchie waitresses: we suspect they're comically inept on purpose.

4 South Great George's Street, Dublin 2.
679 9667

SILK ROAD CAFÉ

Eastern promise

Abraham Phelan certainly has catholic tastes. The Jerusalem native has drawn on the full range of Middle-Eastern influences to create a menu that combines Lebanese and Persian dishes and still finds room for moussaka and cous cous. Situated in the serene surroundings of the Chester Beatty Library, the Silk Road is a hidden gem that offers an uplifting dining experience: The food is healthy! The staff smile at you! Your fellow diners seem like nice people! Walk up to the serving counter, point at whatever takes your fancy and stuff your face with the world's favourite foods. Save room for baklava and coffee. One of our favourite city-centre cafés.

Dublin Castle,
Dublin 2.
407 0770,
silkroadcafe.ie

SIMON'S PLACE

Sweet thing

Every restaurateur calls his dining room 'unique', but Simon's Place is perhaps the only place in the city centre that truly deserves the accolade. There's something about this scruffy little coffee shop that brings a smile to everyone's face. Maybe it's the raggle-taggle decor, the simple, tasty food or the beautiful ladies behind the counter. Head in mid-morning for a freshly-cooked cinnamon bun and a cup of bad but cheap coffee. At lunchtime, it's old-fashioned sandwiches – cheese, chicken, ham, prawn, egg – for only €4.10, with a bowl of thick soup for another €3.50. It's always jammers, but hold out for a window seat and make friends with the people beside you.

22 South Great George's Street, Dublin 2.
679 7821

SOUTH

The Irish Model

We don't know the collective noun for a group of Irish Models, but we bet Clinton White does. As we arrived after a day at the races, the manager was herding a giggling mess of lovelies towards their table. Luckily he still had room for us in the non-fake tan section. This huge venue is usually populated by office workers from the industrial estate that surrounds it, supplemented by cocktail-loving locals. For lunch try the blue cheese and leek tart with pear and walnut salad (€8.95) followed by meatballs al forno with rigatoni, rocket and parmesan (€14.95). At dinner have the beer-battered lemon sole (€23.95). Live music Thursday to Sunday inspires a relaxed lounge vibe.

Blackthorn Road,
Sandyford, Dublin 18.
293 4050, south.ie

THE SOUTH WILLIAM

Eat all the pies

Who can remember life before the South William? We're glad to see that its chilled-out, thrown-together vibe has spread around town over the last couple of years – Shebeen Chic and Hogans' new anonymous bar owe it a certain debt. And like the Shebeen, it was in a bit of a doomed building. Who would've thunk? Anyway, we're cheating slightly by including it here, because it is much more bar than restaurant, but we just *love* their pies. We've tried them all, and we love them all, but if we had to pick it'd be the bacon and cabbage with parsley sauce (€9). Class. Wash it down with one of their very generous glasses of wine; cocktails later on.

52 South William Street, Dublin 2. 672 5946, southwilliam.ie

STILL AT THE DYLAN

Ballsbridge beauty

There was one sunny day in the summer of 2008. We spent it lounging around the Dylan, trying to look like we *belonged*. Social columnists assure us that this is where the beautiful people hang out; alas, not that day. Still, our lunch was beautifully presented, and the waitress was friendly. The dining room exudes a fashionable gaudiness that makes you wish you had a more expensive handbag. We opted for pea and ham soup (€8) and organic free-range chicken with sweetcorn and oyster mushrooms (€15), both lovely and good value considering the postcode. They've just introduced a modern version of afternoon tea (3-5pm) and a lovely tapas menu in the bar (5-7pm).

Eastmoreland Place, Dublin 4. 660 3000, dylan.ie

STOOP YOUR HEAD

Best pub grub

We've never met an unhappy customer of this lovely little pub and restaurant in Skerries. It's welcoming and cosy, with chunky tables packed together and a blackboard announcing the daily specials. You can't book, which means a wait at the bar during busy times (basically always), but the staff is so lovely that no one complains. Since the ocean is mere feet away, chef Andy Davies' menu is all about the seafood, although they do a decent steak too. Start with the chunky chowder (€5.95) or moules marinieres (€7.95), followed by real Dublin Bay prawns fried in butter and garlic (€18.95). Afterwards, say thanks to owner David May down the road in his other venture, Joe May's pub.

Harbour Road, Skerries,
County Dublin.
849 2085

TANTE ZOE'S

Southern belle

Temple Bar, drunk women and loud Cajun music: eating at this Deep South bistro sounds like trying to scratch your brain with a pen knife. Fortunately, three floors mean the parties are usually kept well away from the sober folk. The menu hasn't changed since... ever. Expect plenty of gumbos, jambalayas and blackened this, that and the other. We like dooky gumbo (€6.95), followed by a Lou-Lou Mae jambalaya (€19.50). For afters, the pecan pie is usually a good bet. Cocktails are well-made but even Fintan O'Toole couldn't explain why the sublime Mint Julep is no longer on the list. Perhaps it's because all cocktails must now end in -tini. Anyone for Mint Julep-tini?

1 Crow Street, Temple Bar, Dublin 2. 679 4407, tantezoes.com

THORNTON'S

Prickly rose

Kevin Thornton's trousers got caught in the door one night... and fell off. He kept on cooking, with nary an apron to protect his modesty. His rather sterile restaurant is super-pricey, but the prickly Mr Thornton puts his heart, soul and pants into his cooking. Given the remarkable quality of the ingredients, we think this place offers good value. The great Helen Lucy Burke recalls eating in Thornton's first operation, the Wine Epergne on the Rathmines Road, in 1992. She asked the young chef what mustard he had used on the crubeens. He issued a horrified scream and answered, "Pommery, of course!" We should have known. He was the best then. He is still the best. Go, eat, worship.

128 St Stephen's Green, Dublin 2. 478 7008, thorntonsrestaurant. com

TOWN BAR & GRILL

City slicker

Ronan Ryan deserves credit for each of his restaurants – South and the Bridge are also his – but Town is our favourite. The food (modern Italian) is interesting and well prepared, the wine list is excellent, there is always someone off the telly and the basement dining room is low-lit and intimate (yes it's a basement, but it's a cut above the average dungeon). Start with the lamb's kidney bruschetta (€12.95) and follow with an excellent steak (€29.95) or the fillet of turbot (€34.95). Sunday lunch at €18.95, €24.95 or €29.95 for one, two or three courses is great value. P.S. A reader whinges: "Never again. The piano was too loud." Some people just don't get it.

21 Kildare Street,
Dublin 2. 662 4724,
townbarandgrill.com

THE TROCADERO

Classy lady

One of Dublin's oldest – and most decadent – restaurants remains immune to the recession. You get the impression, in fact, that it will be around for at least another hundred years. For the Troc screams 'Institution.' She's like a rich old friend who is always throwing her house open to thirsty strangers from worlds more tropical than our own. We pitch up late on a Friday night and beg for a seat at the bar, where one inevitably meets some star of stage or screen in a state of disrepair. Waiters are old-school charming, the ambience is red-wall warm, and the maitre d', Robert, is a great host. Dinner only, last orders are at midnight and the food is just okay. (Have the rack of lamb or the cannelloni.)

4 St Andrew Street,
Dublin 2. 677 5545,
trocadero.ie

UKIYO

All-in-one

Duncan McGuire's mantra: "People don't know what they want until you give it to them." How wise. For instance, I didn't know what an amazing singer I was until I drank a bottle of whiskey, hit the karaoke booths in Ukiyo (€25 per hour) and started banging out Tina Turner. Back on ground level, one can enjoy a tranquil lunch, an upbeat dinner or, our favourite, a couple of plates before 11pm, staying on for drinks into the night. Disco Sundays are the latest attraction. The food, both Japanese and Korean, is quite good – try the tuna carpaccio (€12) to start, followed by the beef fillet with sesame and plum sauce (€24). They also do eight kinds of sake. Yikes. Try a small portion of each for €18.50.

7-9 Excheqeur Street, Dublin 2. 633 4071, ukiyobar.com

THE UNICORN

Horny Italian

Signor Casari is the housewives' choice. All glammed up, they descend on this elegant, stylish dining room in the hope that Giorgio will whisper something to them in Italian. Politicians, PRs and publishers are also found loitering in Dublin's answer to the Ivy. Famously, the atmosphere is better than the food, and just as famously, Giorgio refuses to accept as much. In his eyes people love the Unicorn for the generous antipasti buffet, the unremarkable pasta and the veal cutlet with black truffle shavings (now you're talking). Personally I come for Giorgio's wife. Noirin Casari is a lot more fun than most of her customers, and a far more accomplished flirt. No wonder she bagged top prize.

12b Merrion Court,
Dublin 2. 662 4757
unicornrestaurant.com

VERMILION

Curry & lager

There's something inherently shabby about a curry house above a pub. Indeed the modest exterior of the Terenure Inn belies the stylish decor of the restaurant upstairs. Expect fusion cooking – Indian dishes prepared for the bland Irish palate – and fancy loos. Chef Paul Ninan recommends the eral sukka, prawns with ginger, garlic and yoghurt, cooked in a clay oven (€9.95) and fiery gosht mehzabin (€15.95) for mains. The bill can quickly mount up here, although it's possible to get good value midweek – two courses and a bottle of wine cost €60 for two people – and while portions are large, it's now possible to order smaller portions at reduced prices. Open for dinner only, jazz on Friday nights.

94-96 Terenure Road North, Dublin 6W. 499 1400, vermilion.ie

WAGAMAMA

Use your noodle

One might imagine that restaurants are all like this in Tokyo – efficient, funky, minimalist. They are not. Still, this branch of the international chain is a brilliant spot for a city-centre lunch, as long as you're not planning on firing/breaking up/ telling the person you're with that you're pregnant. (Shared tables. Benches. Sore arse.) You'll be in and out comfortably within the hour, without feeling like there's a big rush on. On a menu full of ramen, teppan, noodles etc, we like the yaki udon (€13.45), noodles with prawns, chicken, salmon, eggs and lots of other bits, with duck gyoza dumplings to start (€8.35). Plus: very delicious raw juice that will leave you feeling hyper-virtuous.

South King Street,
Dublin 2. 478 2152,
wagamama.ie

WILDE

Oscar winner

Real-life Dubs still man the erstwhile Russell Room, now joined by a couple of distaff Europeans. After an elaborate redecoration, the space itself – arguably the best location in the city – looks chic. At night the lighting is rather dark. In the daytime it looks terrific. Ignore the two-course lunch menu (€25) with its generic international fare. The two best things a la carte are the Caesar salad and the grilled lobster. The Caesar is made at the table. Much ado. The lobster is huge, and a selection of butter sauces and boiled new potatoes are a fine complement. Side dishes (all €5) include fine hand-cut chips with sea salt and onion rings in a cider batter. P.S Excellent aged steaks too.

Grafton Street,
Dublin 2.
646 3311
wilderestaurant.com

THE WILD GOOSE

Exciting addition

Kevin McMahon, who ran Ely wine bar for seven years, says he wanted "to create a nice, smart, comfortable wine bistro – more old-fashioned, perhaps, than some of the places in a village that feels increasingly slick." He has succeeded. The interior of this first-floor dining room above McSorleys is most handsome. The service is enthusiastic, and the wine list is quite superb. One might start with a big bowl of mussels (€10), then share the popular steak for two, carved at your table. Both delicious. Or else have pappardelle with mild mushrooms and great big cloves of roast garlic (€16). The Wild Goose represents a serious challenge to the competition in Ranelagh. It deserves to thrive.

1 Sandford Road, Dublin 6. 491 2377

Some things are missing here...

Santa Rita is
one of them.

Santa Rita
Savour the Moment

www.santarita.com

THE WINDING STAIR

Worth the climb

"**On the wrong** side of the Liffey. Up two flights of stairs. And more importantly: up its own arse." That's one reader's verdict on the Winding Stair. A little harsh? Indeed. Manager Elaine Murphy is a pro, and this tiny operation is rightly acclaimed as one of the city's more exciting newcomers. Yes, there is a lot of nonsense about booking tables, and yes, you may find yourself wondering what all the fuss was about when you see the modest dining room. But there is no denying the talent in the kitchen. This is one of the few restaurants in the city that might accurately be described as a showcase for modern Irish cooking. And nothing is particularly expensive.

40 Ormond Quay,
Dublin 1. 872 7320,
winding-stair.com

WONGS

Suburban Chinese

A couple with two children is berating a uniformed Chinese man sporting a large smiley-face badge as we enter Castleknock's most lauded Asian restaurant. Apparently the management asked them if their kids stuck chewing gum underneath the table. A uniformed waitress (also wearing a large smiley-face badge) is saying that there was no-one at the table before them and there was no chewing gum either. There is now. The parents feign shock. The manager tries to defuse the situation with a wry smile. It doesn't work. Eventually the couple leaves, indicating that this will not be the end of the matter. Who would be a restaurateur? (Other than that, the Cantonese duck is fine. Just fine.)

Ashleigh Centre,
Main Street,
Castleknock, Dublin 15.
822 3330

YAMAMORI

Yummy yummy

Manager Jenny Griffin says Blondie order takeaway from here when they are in town. We'd advise them to eat in instead – it's great fun. Bring a group of friends early on a Friday night. Insist on one of the booths – they seem to be saving them for Fukuda. (Or the new bloke.) Start with some sake and the large sushi plate (10 pieces of the chef's selection, €22) for the table. After that, we like the yaki soba, noodles with chicken, pork, seafood and other bits (€9.90) or the ramen. The tempura has its good and bad days. There's a great expanded garden out the back for smokers. The kimonoed waitresses have a faraway look in their eyes – try to cheer them up.

71-72 South Great George's Street, Dublin 2. 475 5001, yamamorinoodles.ie

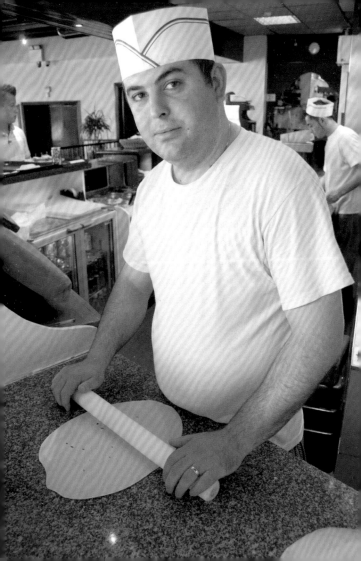

ZAYTOON

Perfect Persian

I spent two weeks travelling around Iran. Everywhere I went, people offered me kebabs. Unfortunately they offered me very little else. I wanted to like Persian cooking, but I was carrying a bit of baggage around that made it impossible to appreciate the food. You see, I love Zaytoon. This fast-food joint boasts a menu that is shorter than Bertie's Guide to Proper English, yet it remains a haven for anyone who loves a good kebab. The signature dish is chicken shish – marinated boneless chicken fillet grilled in a clay oven (€9.70). But the best thing to eat is the barg (€11.70) – tender beef, garlic sauce and lovely fresh oven-baked bread. A pleasant experience, even when sober.

44-45 Lower Camden Street, Dublin 2. 400 5006

WHAT DO YOU WANT TO EAT?

IRISH

FRENCH

ASIAN

ITALIAN

MODERN EUROPEAN

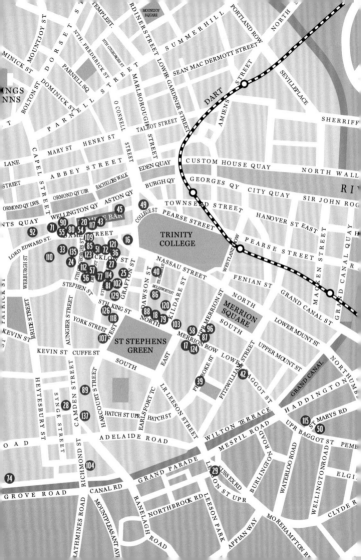

SOUTH CITY

NORTH DUBLIN

NORTH CITY

NEW ENTRIES...

...NEW EXITS

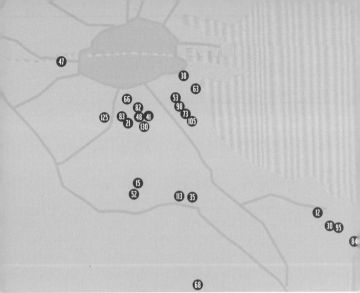

SOUTH DUBLIN

ACKNOWLEDGEMENTS

The editor wishes to acknowledge the support of Salvador Domenech at Santa Rita and Terry Pennington, Julia Kennedy, Maureen O'Hara and their colleagues at Gilbeys of Ireland Ltd, the distributors of Santa Rita wines in Ireland.

A dozen journalists contribute to the restaurant pages in *The Dubliner* magazine. Fearless eaters and shrewd judges, their number includes Helen Lucy Burke, Eoin Higgins, Richard Lubell, Derek Owens, Emily Hourican and Paul Trainer.

The staff of the magazine, in particular Art Director Fiachra McCarthy, Deputy Editor Nicola Reddy and Publishing Manager Paul Trainer, contribute a great deal to the success of the guide. Tiffany Reagan, Constance Parpoil, Nicholas Hamilton, Richard Ashcroft, Emma Jane Gallagher and Amy Roe all assisted in production. The photography is by Yuri Igoshev and Giita Hammond. *The Dubliner 100 Best Restaurants* was proofread by Dona Le and Sarah Osborne.

TREVOR WHITE was educated at Sandford Park, St Columba's and Trinity College, before stints in London, Prague, New York and Bermuda. He became Features Editor of *Food and Wine* in 1997. Today White is the editor of *The Dubliner* magazine. His book, *Kitchen Con: Writing on the Restaurant Racket*, was published in 2006. The first edition of *The Dubliner 100 Best Bars* was published in 2007. This is the seventh edition of *The Dubliner 100 Best Restaurants*.